MW01196542

If found please return to:

_____

_____

_____

_____

TRAIL

Date [   ] Rating

Start time & point

End time & point

Weather

Plants & Animals

My favorite part was...

Scavenger Hunt

2 Types of Seed or Nut	Feather
Spider Web	Animal Scat
Pine Needles	Something that makes noise
Mushroom	Animal Track
Bird	2 Types of Leaves

TRAIL

Date _____ Rating

Start time & point

End time & point

Weather

Plants & Animals

My favorite part was...

Scavenger Hunt

	2 Types of Seed or Nut		Feather
	Spider Web		Animal Scat
	Pine Needles		Something that makes noise
	Mushroom		Animal Track
	Bird		2 Types of Leaves

TRAIL

Date **[**   **]**   Rating

Start time & point   End time & point

Weather

Plants & Animals

My favorite part was...

Scavenger Hunt

2 Types of Seed or Nut	**Feather**
Spider Web	**Animal Scat**
Pine Needles	**Something that makes noise**
Mushroom	**Animal Track**
Bird	**2 Types of Leaves**

TRAIL

Date _____   Rating ⟍ ⟍ ⟍ ⟍ ⟍

Start time & point   End time & point

Weather

Plants & Animals

My favorite part was...

Scavenger Hunt

2 Types of Seed or Nut	Feather
Spider Web	Animal Scat
Pine Needles	Something that makes noise
Mushroom	Animal Track
Bird	2 Types of Leaves

TRAIL

Date _____

Rating

Start time & point

End time & point

Weather

Plants & Animals

My favorite part was...

Scavenger Hunt

| 2 Types of Seed or Nut | Feather |

| Spider Web | Animal Scat |

| Pine Needles | Something that makes noise |

| Mushroom | Animal Track |

| Bird | 2 Types of Leaves |

TRAIL

Date [   ] Rating

Start time & point   End time & point

[   ]

Weather

Plants & Animals

My favorite part was...

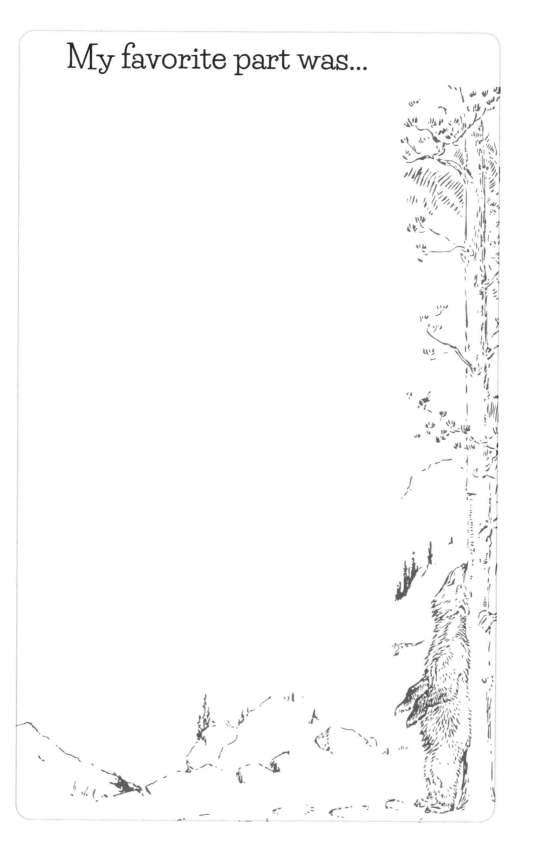

Scavenger Hunt

2 Types of Seed or Nut	Feather
Spider Web	Animal Scat
Pine Needles	Something that makes noise
Mushroom	Animal Track
Bird	2 Types of Leaves

TRAIL

Date ( ) Rating

Start time & point   End time & point

Weather

Plants & Animals

My favorite part was...

Scavenger Hunt

2 Types of Seed or Nut	**Feather**
Spider Web	**Animal Scat**
Pine Needles	**Something that makes noise**
Mushroom	**Animal Track**
Bird	**2 Types of Leaves**

TRAIL

Date [   ] Rating

Start time & point

End time & point

Weather

Plants & Animals

My favorite part was...

Scavenger Hunt

2 Types of Seed or Nut

Feather

Spider Web

Animal Scat

Pine Needles

Something that makes noise

Mushroom

Animal Track

Bird

2 Types of Leaves

TRAIL

Date [   ] Rating

Start time & point   End time & point

Weather

Plants & Animals

My favorite part was...

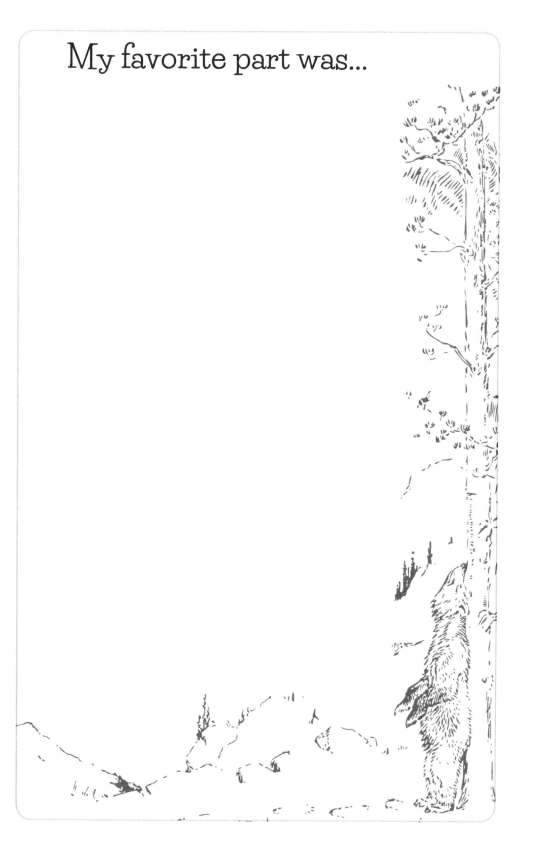

Scavenger Hunt

2 Types of Seed or Nut	Feather
Spider Web	Animal Scat
Pine Needles	Something that makes noise
Mushroom	Animal Track
Bird	2 Types of Leaves

TRAIL

Date [ ] Rating

Start time & point   End time & point

Weather

Plants & Animals

My favorite part was...

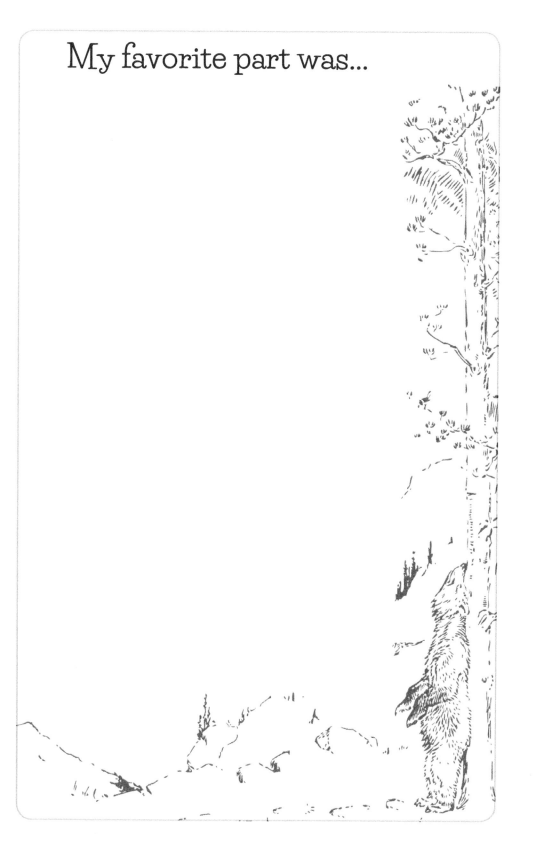

Scavenger Hunt

2 Types of Seed or Nut

Feather

Spider Web

Animal Scat

Pine Needles

Something that makes noise

Mushroom

Animal Track

Bird

2 Types of Leaves

TRAIL

Date [_____] Rating

Start time & point   End time & point

Weather

Plants & Animals

My favorite part was...

Scavenger Hunt

	2 Types of Seed or Nut		**Feather**

	Spider Web		**Animal Scat**

	Pine Needles		**Something that makes noise**

	Mushroom		**Animal Track**

	Bird		**2 Types of Leaves**

TRAIL

Date _____   Rating

Start time & point   End time & point

Weather

Plants & Animals

My favorite part was...

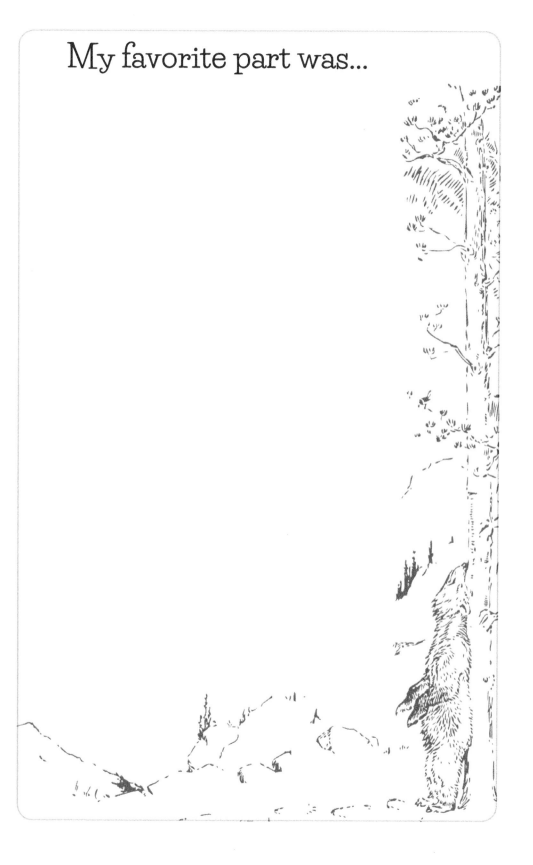

Scavenger Hunt

2 Types of Seed or Nut	Feather
Spider Web	Animal Scat
Pine Needles	Something that makes noise
Mushroom	Animal Track
Bird	2 Types of Leaves

TRAIL

Date [   ]   Rating

Start time & point   End time & point

Weather

Plants & Animals

My favorite part was...

Scavenger Hunt

2 Types of Seed or Nut	Feather
Spider Web	Animal Scat
Pine Needles	Something that makes noise
Mushroom	Animal Track
Bird	2 Types of Leaves

TRAIL

Date _____ Rating

Start time & point   End time & point

Weather

Plants & Animals

My favorite part was...

Scavenger Hunt

2 Types of Seed or Nut	**Feather**
Spider Web	**Animal Scat**
Pine Needles	**Something that makes noise**
Mushroom	**Animal Track**
Bird	**2 Types of Leaves**

TRAIL

Date _____   Rating

Start time & point   End time & point

Weather

Plants & Animals

My favorite part was...

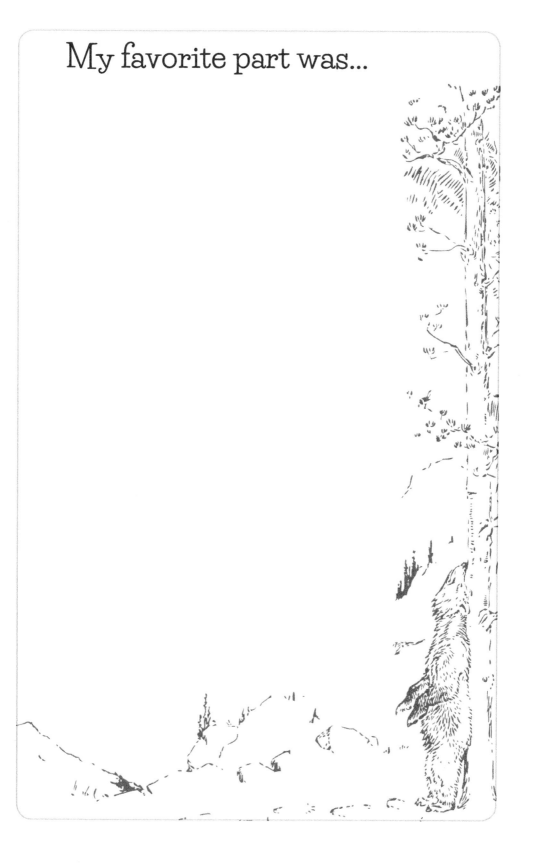

Scavenger Hunt

2 Types of Seed or Nut	**Feather**
Spider Web	**Animal Scat**
Pine Needles	**Something that makes noise**
Mushroom	**Animal Track**
Bird	**2 Types of Leaves**

TRAIL

Date [   ] Rating

Start time & point   End time & point

Weather

Plants & Animals

My favorite part was...

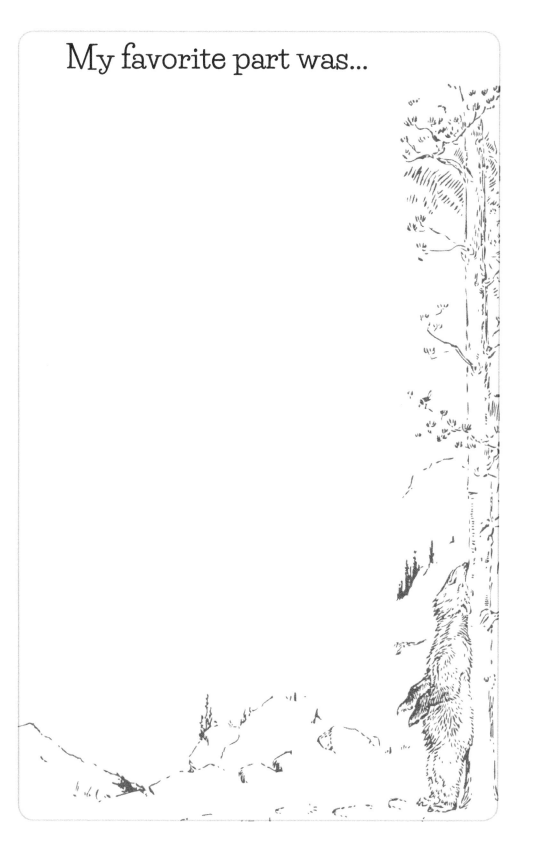

Scavenger Hunt

2 Types of Seed or Nut	Feather
Spider Web	Animal Scat
Pine Needles	Something that makes noise
Mushroom	Animal Track
Bird	2 Types of Leaves

TRAIL

Date _____ Rating

Start time & point   End time & point

Weather

Plants & Animals

My favorite part was...

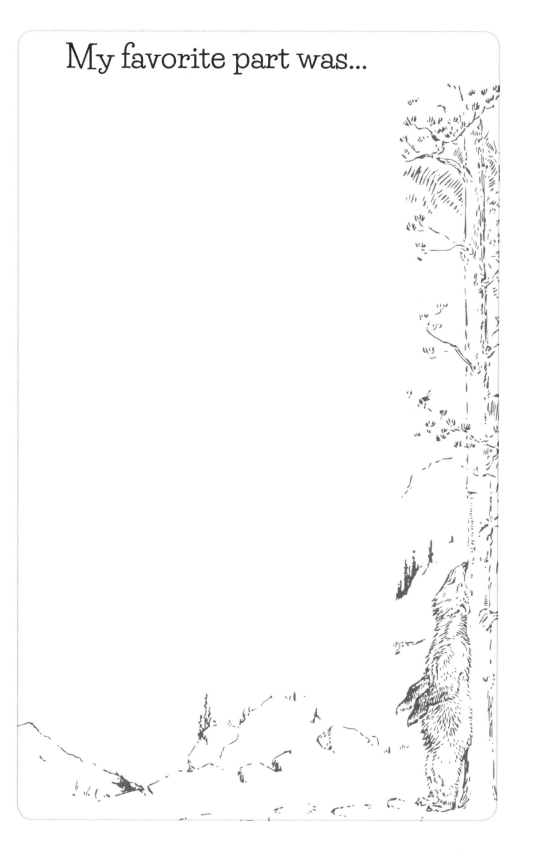

Scavenger Hunt

2 Types of Seed or Nut	Feather
Spider Web	Animal Scat
Pine Needles	Something that makes noise
Mushroom	Animal Track
Bird	2 Types of Leaves

TRAIL

Date [   ] Rating

Start time & point   End time & point

Weather

Plants & Animals

My favorite part was...

Scavenger Hunt

2 Types of Seed or Nut	**Feather**
Spider Web	**Animal Scat**
Pine Needles	**Something that makes noise**
Mushroom	**Animal Track**
Bird	**2 Types of Leaves**

TRAIL

Date [   ]   Rating

Start time & point   End time & point

Weather

Plants & Animals

My favorite part was...

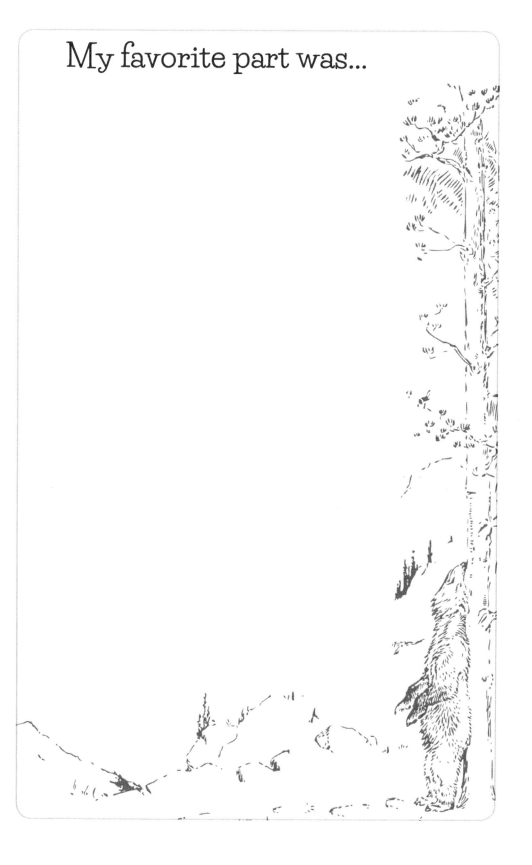

Scavenger Hunt

2 Types of Seed or Nut	**Feather**
Spider Web	**Animal Scat**
Pine Needles	**Something that makes noise**
Mushroom	**Animal Track**
Bird	**2 Types of Leaves**

TRAIL

Date [ ] Rating

Start time & point

End time & point

Weather

Plants & Animals

My favorite part was...

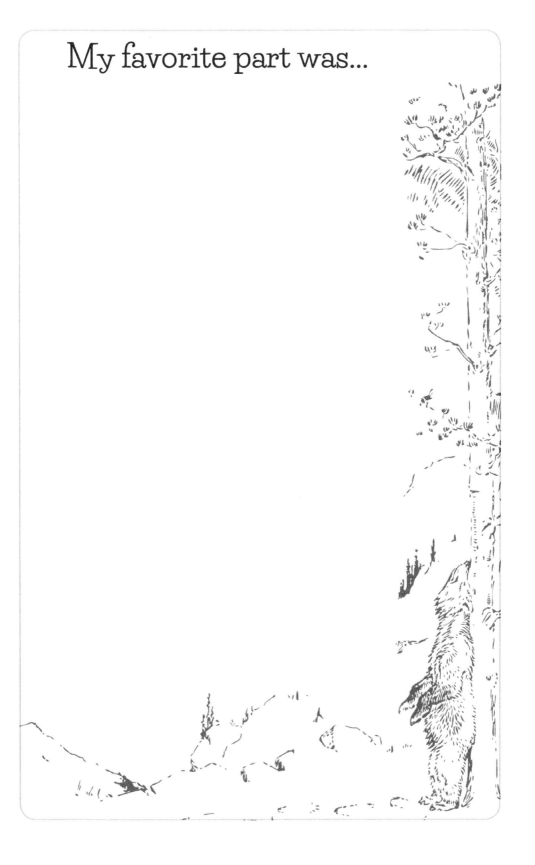

Scavenger Hunt

2 Types of Seed or Nut	Feather
Spider Web	Animal Scat
Pine Needles	Something that makes noise
Mushroom	Animal Track
Bird	2 Types of Leaves

TRAIL

Date [   ]   Rating

Start time & point   End time & point

Weather

Plants & Animals

My favorite part was...

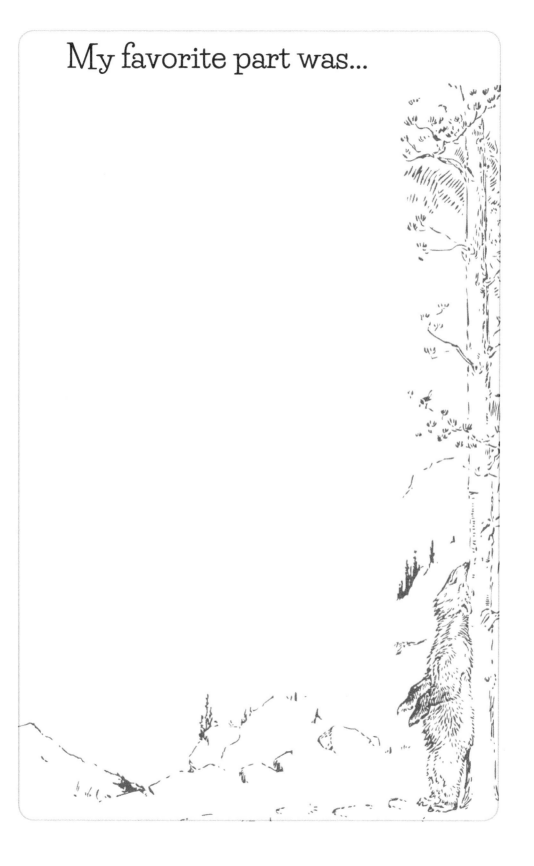

Scavenger Hunt

2 Types of Seed or Nut	**Feather**
Spider Web	**Animal Scat**
Pine Needles	**Something that makes noise**
Mushroom	**Animal Track**
Bird	**2 Types of Leaves**

TRAIL

Date [ ] Rating

Start time & point   End time & point

Weather

Plants & Animals

My favorite part was...

Scavenger Hunt

2 Types of Seed or Nut	Feather
Spider Web	Animal Scat
Pine Needles	Something that makes noise
Mushroom	Animal Track
Bird	2 Types of Leaves

TRAIL

Date [   ]   Rating

Start time & point   End time & point

Weather

Plants & Animals

My favorite part was...

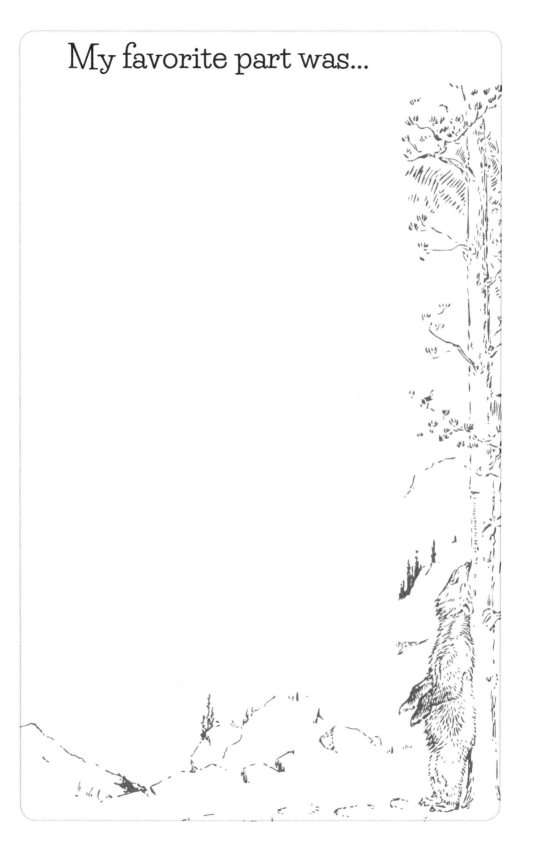

Scavenger Hunt

2 Types of Seed or Nut	**Feather**
Spider Web	**Animal Scat**
Pine Needles	**Something that makes noise**
Mushroom	**Animal Track**
Bird	**2 Types of Leaves**

TRAIL

Date [   ]   Rating 👢👢👢👢👢

Start time & point   End time & point

Weather

Plants & Animals

My favorite part was...

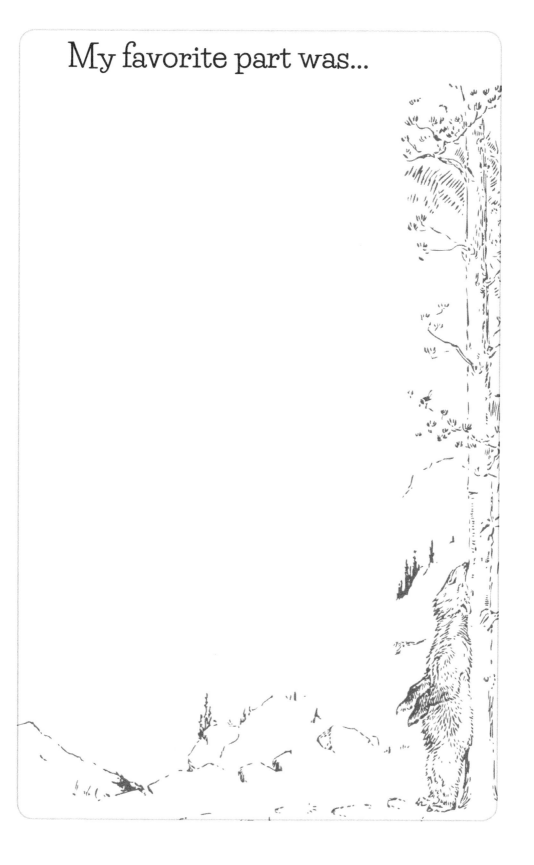

Scavenger Hunt

2 Types of Seed or Nut

Feather

Spider Web

Animal Scat

Pine Needles

Something that makes noise

Mushroom

Animal Track

Bird

2 Types of Leaves

Made in the USA
Coppell, TX
17 March 2022

74983767R00057